Why Do Cats Do That?

By Nancy White • illustrated by Gioia Fiammenghi

Scholastic Inc.
New York Toronto London Auckland Sydney

Dedication/Acknowledgments

To Jeoffry, Fluffy, and Marmalade . . . and their humans —*NW*

To Elena, with love —*Gioia*

Acknowledgment

To Dr. Karen Overall at the School of Veterinary Medicine of the University of Pennsylvania, I offer most sincere thanks for sharing your expertise and fascinating insights into the world of cats and why they do the things they do. Your suggestions, corrections, and additions to the manuscript worked to the great advantage of this book.

ISBN 0-590-95942-5

12 11 10 9 8 7 6 5 4 3   7 8 9/9 0 1 2/0

Printed in the U.S.A.

First Scholastic printing, July 1997

Book design by Laurie Williams

Contents

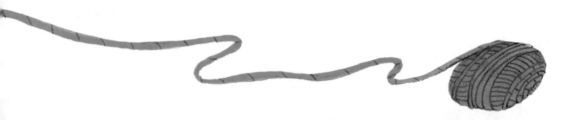

Dear Readers,

    Some of the questions in this book were asked by kids. Some were asked by grown-ups. Cat owners asked some of the questions, and people who don't even have a cat asked questions, too. I guess cats do such amazing things that lots of people want to know more about them.

    I hope this book answers some of *your* questions about cats and why they do the amazing things they do.

    Sincerely,

Nancy White

Nancy White

Are Lions and Tigers Really Cats?

Yes, they really are! Lions, tigers, mountain lions, jaguars, cheetahs, and leopards are all members of the cat family. They are your cat's wild relatives. Even the friendliest, gentlest little cats are in many ways like their wild cousins.

All those wild members of the cat family live on their own and hunt for their food. Pet cats live with people and eat food that comes from the store.

BUT—all cats, even pets, can be expert hunters if they want to or need to be. They are fast runners and high jumpers. They have great eyesight, and they can walk very quietly. Can you see why cats are such good hunters?

Can Cats and Dogs Be Friends?

Cats and dogs are a little like people who speak different languages, so they often have a hard time understanding each other. For example, a low-pitched sound a dog makes in her throat is a growl. That means "Stay away." But when a cat makes a low-pitched sound in his throat, it's a purr!

Here's another example. Dogs sometimes show friendliness by wagging their tails. But cats don't wag their tails unless they're feeling nervous!

But dogs and cats can learn to understand each other if they live together. They can even get to be best friends!

Why Do Cats Purr?

Kittens purr to let their mother know that every-thing's okay. When a mother cat hears her kittens purring, she knows she doesn't need to worry about them.

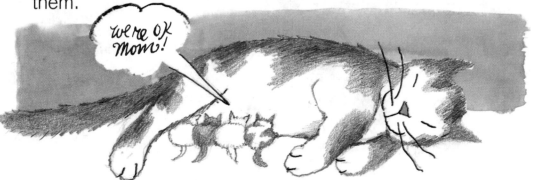

Adult cats purr when they feel safe and happy.

Cats can purr for a long time without stopping. Why don't they have to stop to take a breath? Because they purr while breathing both in and out.

Why Do Cats Meow?

Pretend this is a dictionary of cat language.
Here are four different meanings for "meow":

I'm hungry.

I want to go out.

Help!

I want attention!

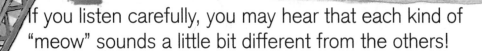

If you listen carefully, you may hear that each kind of
"meow" sounds a little bit different from the others!

9

Why Does a Cat's Tongue Feel Rough?

If you've ever been licked by a cat, you probably know that a cat's tongue is as rough as sandpaper. Cats use their rough tongues to brush their fur and keep it smooth.

Cats' tongues are so rough, they can use them to scrape meat off bones! (This comes in handy, especially for cats in the wild.)

Why Do Cats Lick Themselves So Much?

A few reasons:

- Licking keeps a cat's fur clean and smooth.

- Licking cools a cat off in hot weather.

- Licking helps a cat's fur stay waterproof.

- Licking fluffs up a cat's fur. Fluffy fur is better for keeping a cat warm.

- If a cat hurts himself, licking the cut or scratch cleans it and helps it feel better.

Why Do Cats Love It When You Scratch Behind Their Ears?

Because that's the only place they can't lick! (But they do wash behind their ears with their front paws.)

Why Do Cats Like to Be Petted?

A mother cat licks her kittens to keep them clean. A kitten feels happy and safe while his mother is taking care of him.

To your cat, petting feels a lot like licking. When you pet your cat slowly and gently, he knows you are taking good care of him. You're showing that you love him.

What Does It Mean When a Cat Arches Her Back and Puffs Up?

This cat is scared or angry. Or maybe she's scared *and* angry.

If you were scared, wouldn't you like to look like a giant? That's what a cat is doing when she arches her back and puffs up her fur. A big scary dog or another cat might think she's much bigger than she really is.

Another way cats make themselves look bigger is to stand sideways. Pretty good trick!

If a cat hisses or growls, that means she's angry, too. Better stay away!

Why Do Cats Press Against You With Their Paws?

Kittens get milk by nursing from their mother. They press against their mother with first one paw and then the other. This is called "kneading" or "treading." Kneading helps the mother cat give milk to the kittens.

When an adult cat kneads or treads with his paws, it makes him feel like a happy little kitten.

Why Do Cats Sometimes Roll Over on Their Backs When They See You?

This is one of the friendliest things a cat can do. It's her way of saying she trusts you.

Why Do Cats Rub Up Against Your Legs?

The more you smell like a cat, the more a cat likes being around you. When a cat rubs up against you, she's getting some of her own smell on you. Also, she's letting other cats know you are her own special friend.

Don't worry! You'll only smell like a cat to a cat. Humans won't know the difference.

In the wild, lions rub faces with each other to "introduce" themselves or show they want to be friendly.

Why Do Cats Sometimes Knock Things Over?

If your cat jumps on a shelf or table and knocks something off, it's not an accident! This might be her idea of fun. And if you chase her, she'll think that's fun, too.

Or she might be trying to get you to pay attention to her.

Why Do Cats Climb Trees?

Mainly for protection. By running up a tree, a cat can get away from an animal that is chasing her.

Another reason is that sitting in a tree gives a cat a good view. She can see what other animals are around, or keep an eye on what's going on in the neighborhood. Even indoor cats like high places— like the top of the refrigerator or a high bookshelf.

Cats have very strong muscles in their hind legs. Also, their hind legs are longer than their front legs. Those long, strong hind legs can really get a cat off the ground!

Do Cats Really Always Land on Their Feet?

Not always, but more often than most other animals.

Cats like to climb up to high places. They're very good at keeping their balance, but sometimes they fall. When they do, they can twist, turn, and balance their bodies so that they land on their feet.

If a cat has time to spread out his front and back legs, he falls more slowly, because his body acts as a parachute. Cats' tails help them balance, too.

But sometimes cats do get hurt when they fall, so if you have a cat, don't take chances!

Why Do Cats Sometimes Make Mad Dashes Around the House?

When your cat makes a mad dash around the house for no reason, don't worry. He's not crazy. He's just using up energy.

Nature gave cats lots of energy to chase other animals—and run away when they're being chased. Your pet cat doesn't have to do these things at home. But he has fun pretending he's wild.

I just gotta run

Why Do Some Cats Kill Mice and Birds?

In the wild, cats have to hunt for their own food. Nobody buys kitty treats for lions or tigers.

Hunting means chasing another animal, killing it, and eating it. Don't think cats are mean because they go after mice, birds, or rabbits. Try thinking of your cat as a little lion or tiger that happens to live in a house. That's how your cat thinks of herself!

How Come Most Cats Don't Eat a Lot of Food at Once?

The natural amount of food for a cat to eat at one time is just about equal to one mouse! And that's not much.

After one mouseworth of cat food, a cat feels full. He'll eat a little bit, but he'll want to come back and eat again before too long.

Why Does a Cat Always Seem to Want to Come In Right After You Let Him Out?

He's not trying to drive you crazy! He's just acting like his wild relatives. A wild cat has his own special place to hunt. He feels like he owns that place, and he doesn't like other animals coming around.

A pet cat feels like his yard is his own special place. Every once in a while he likes to check out who else might be around. After that, he wants to come back in where it's safe and warm.

Why Do Cats Like to Go Out at Night?

For cats, nighttime is a good time for hunting. And they are able to get along well in the dark.

No animal can see if there's no light at all. But cats can see if there's just the tiniest bit of light. The pupils of a cat's eyes can open very wide to let in lots of light.

Also, a cat's eye reflects light like a mirror. Even a very tiny dim light seems much brighter. That's why a cat's eyes seem to glow in the dark.

A cat's whiskers help her at night, too. They are not just for decoration!

If a cat can get through a space without her whiskers touching, she knows the rest of her body will go through the space, too—even if it's too dark to see.

Every cat has 24 whiskers, 12 on each side. When cats are curious, they hold their whiskers forward. When they are scared, they hold their whiskers back against the face.

Why Do Cats Scratch People Sometimes?

When a cat scratches a person, he's probably annoyed, angry, or scared. He's just trying to defend himself. But it sure can hurt!

Here are a few of the things that annoy or scare a cat:

- pulling his tail

- squeezing him

- grabbing him (especially if you're a stranger)

- trying to dress him up in baby clothes

Any of these things might make a cat want to scratch you, so don't do them. Remember that a cat is a living animal, not a toy. Handle cats gently, and respect their feelings!

Why Do Some Cats Claw the Furniture?

People, especially grown-ups, hate this habit. But some cats do it anyway. Here are four reasons:

• It sharpens their claws.

• It exercises their claw muscles.

• It helps scrape off the old outside covering of each claw. (There is a fresh new covering underneath.)

• Your cat uses his paws to get his own special smell on things around your house!

If you give your cat a scratching post when he's a young kitten, he might learn to leave the furniture alone.

Cats use special muscles to pull their claws in and push them out. When the claws go in, they slide into little "pockets" in the cat's toes. The cat can walk without making a sound. When a cat needs her claws for climbing, hunting, defending herself, or clawing the sofa, they come out again.

What Toys Do Cats Like to Play With?

Anything small and soft that moves easily. Cats like to swat their toys around and pounce on them.

Your cat is having fun when she plays. She's also getting in her hunting practice. When your cat pounces on a toy (or your toes), she's pretending to hunt. She's showing her wild side.

Why Do Cats Love Catnip?

Catnip is a plant. Most cats just love the way it smells. Catnip leaves are dried and used to stuff cat toys. Catnip also comes in a can to spray on toys or a cat's scratching post.

Do Cats Watch TV?

Sometimes cats really look like they're watching TV!
They're not paying attention to the story, though.
And they don't care who wins the World Series,
either. What they like is the flickering motion they
see on the screen.

Cats love to watch anything that moves. That's why
they like to stare at drops of rain trickling down the
windowpane. Or a string that you pull along the
floor. Or your pencil when you're trying to do your
homework.

Most hunting animals are interested in things that
move. Why do you think that is?

Can You Train a Cat to Do Tricks?

Cats are not dogs, so they probably won't want to do all the same tricks that dogs do.

But cats can be trained to understand many human words and commands. They can learn tricks, too, if you reward them with food treats. Some cats can learn to retrieve a ball, ring the doorbell, or turn on the water faucet and take a drink!

that must be Shadow

Can Cats Tell Time?

You never saw a cat wearing a watch, did you? But your cat might seem to know when someone in your family is coming home—even before you do. Or she might seem to know when it's feeding time, or when you're about to wake up in the morning.

Cats can't tell time the way people can, but they get to know the habits and routines of their families. They learn just what to expect—and when—without ever looking at a clock!

When Does a Kitten Become a Cat?

Here is a "calendar" of important events in the first year of a kitten's life:

KITTY CALENDAR

•**One Day Old:** Newborn kittens are tiny. You can hold them in the palm of your hand. They can't see or hear, but they can smell. About all they do is sleep and drink milk from their mother.

•**One Week Old:** The kittens' eyes begin to open. They weigh twice as much as they did when they were born.

•**One Month Old:** The kittens can sit up. They start playing together. → Lick milk from bowl & eat kitten food from the store

•**Two Months Old:** The kittens stop nursing from their mother and start eating food. They start really playing rough!

•**Three Months Old:** The kittens lose their baby teeth and start getting their second teeth.

• **Six Months Old:** The kittens can get along on their own.

• **One Year Old:** The kittens are full-grown cats.

Cats live to be about 14 years old, but many live to be 20 or even older.

Why Are Some Cats Friendlier Than Others?

The friendliest cats are the ones who got used to being with people when they were very young kittens.

If you want a friendly kitten, try to choose one that is used to being picked up and petted. If your cat has kittens, handle them very gently and lovingly. You can talk softly to them, too. (Say whatever you want. The kittens won't know the difference!)

If your cat is shy, don't try to pet him or hold him until he's ready. And don't chase him. Just talk to him softly and be patient. He'll get to know you after a while.

The Cat Who Goes to School

Woody is a big, friendly, orange-colored cat, with white paws and a white chest. Woody spends most days sleeping, eating, being petted, and playing with his favorite toys—an orange stuffed-animal cat and a stuffed mouse with bells on it.

But Wednesday is a special day for Woody. That's the day he goes to school! Woody spends every Wednesday in Mrs. Case's first-grade classroom at Northfield Elementary School in Northfield, Ohio. The kids in the class take turns taking care of Woody. They draw pictures of him. And they write stories about the funny things he does—such as unrolling all the toilet paper in the bathroom, and knocking over the book easel, sending books flying all over the place! And if you're feeling sad and Woody comes over to play, or just sit on your desk, it makes you feel better!

Mrs. Case found Woody during a thunderstorm when he was only twelve weeks old. She thought he would make a good classroom cat because he was so friendly. But first, Woody had to pass a test. During his test, Woody looked back at people when they looked at him, he let strangers pick him up and hold him, and he didn't get scared by the loud noise of a dish falling on the floor. Then he got a name tag that says he is an official "Pet Partner." Now Woody is five years old, and he's been going to school since he was two. Each year, Mrs. Case makes sure no one is allergic to cats, and teaches the kids how to take care of a cat before Woody joins the class.

One year Mrs. Case's class built Woody his own "Kitty Condo" out of cardboard boxes. Then they made him his own special blanket. All the girls and boys learned how to knit! Each one knitted a square out of yarn. When all the squares were finished, they were sewn together to make Woody's blanket.

The kids in Mrs. Case's class really love Woody. He gets to be in the class picture, and on Valentine's Day, he gets the most valentines of anyone!